Schwerpunktthema

Abitur Englisch

Ray Bradbury: Two Short Stories

The Veldt and The Murderer

Cornelsen

Ray Bradbury: Two Short Stories
"The Veldt" and "The Murderer"

Herausgegeben von

Ulrich Imig

Verlagsredaktion

Neil Porter

Layout und technische Umsetzung

Buchgestaltung+, Berlin

Umschlaggestaltung

havemannundmosch, bureau für gestaltung, Berlin

Bildquellen:

Pp. 17–18 charts 1, 2 and 3: © The Henry J. Kaiser Family Foundation; p. 18 bottom: © Bob Englehart – All Rights Reserved; p. 26 top: Museum für Kommunikation, Frankfurt am Main; p. 26 bottom: © Uwe Kraft Fotografie, Düsseldorf; p. 30 top: Shutterstock images, New York (© Pavel Losevsky); p. 30 bottom: © Xinhua/Das Fotoarchiv; p. 32 all: © action press / SOUTH WEST NEWS SERVICE; p. 35: Alamy images (© Ethno Images/Pierre Roussel).

www.cornelsen.de

1. Auflage, 1. Druck 2009

Alle Drucke dieser Auflage sind inhaltlich unverändert und können im Unterricht nebeneinander verwendet werden.

Druck: CS-Druck CornelsenStürtz, Berlin

ISBN 978-3-06-031262-7

Inhalt gedruckt auf säurefreiem Papier aus nachhaltiger Forstwirtschaft.

Contents

Abbreviations and symbols

adj	adjective
abbr	abbreviation
AE	American English
cf.	confer, see
derog	derogatory
ed.	editor
e.g.	(Latin) exempli gratia = for example
esp.	especially
etc.	(Latin) et cetera = and so on
ff.	and the following lines/pages
fml	formal
i.e.	(Latin) id est = that is
infml	informal
l., ll.	line, lines
lit	literary
n	noun
p., pp.	page, pages
pl	plural
sb.	somebody
sl	slang
sth.	something
usu.	usually
v	verb
vulg	vulgar

Getting Started

This book contains two stories: "The Veldt" (first published 1952 in *The Illustrated Man*) and "The Murderer" (first published 1953 in *The Golden Apples of the Sun*). Both stories deal with the influence of media on interpersonal relationships or an individual's well-being. They were written by Ray Bradbury, who was born in Waukegan, Illinois, in 1920, and who is regarded as one of the finest American science-fiction writers. His most famous work is *Fahrenheit 451* (1953). In his work Bradbury often depicts future societies in which tendencies of the present age have been taken to a further degree.

Before you read the stories, read the following tasks below:

1 Define the term "science fiction". Explain the relationship between the fictional world which has been created in a science-fiction story and the contemporary reality in which the story was written.

2 a) Make a mental tour through your house and list all the gadgets used to do household chores. Categorize them as either indispensable, useful or unnecessary. Compare and discuss your lists.
  b) Describe what life was like before each particular gadget was invented.
  c) Present your lists to your parents and grandparents. Interview them about their view of what is necessary or not. Report your findings to the class.

3 Think of technological innovations and potential improvements of already existing gadgets and media,
  - which seem likely,
  - which, according to you, are desirable.

4 You and your gadgets. Find out how important electronic media are to you by filling in the questionnaire on the following page. (You can, of course, modify the questionnaire.)

How much time per week do you spend:

Using the following devices	Hours spent
watching TV	
watching DVDs	
listening to the radio	
listening to your CD-player	
listening to your mp3 player	
using your computer for text processing	
using your computer for internet surfing	
using your computer for internet research	
using your computer for chatting or phoning	
using your computer for e-mailing	
playing with games (on your computer or play station, etc.)	
reading traditional print media	
using your mobile phone	

Compare your results with a partner.
What would you say is the most important device for you? And why?

The Veldt

"George, I wish you'd look at the nursery."

"What's wrong with it?"

"I don't know."

"Well, then."

"I just want you to look at it, is all, or call a psychologist in to look at it."

"What would a psychologist want with a nursery?"

"You know very well what he'd want." His wife paused in the middle of the kitchen and watched the stove busy humming to itself, making supper for four.

"It's just that the nursery is different now than it was."

"All right, let's have a look."

They walked down the hall of their soundproofed, Happy-life Home, which had cost them thirty thousand dollars installed, this house which clothed and fed and rocked them to sleep and played and sang and was good to them. Their approach sensitized a switch somewhere and the nursery light flicked on when they came within ten feet of it. Similarly, behind them, in the halls, lights went on and off as they left them behind, with a soft automaticity.

"Well," said George Hadley.

They stood on the thatched floor of the nursery. It was forty feet across by forty feet long and thirty feet high; it had cost half again as much as the rest of the house. "But nothing's too good for our children," George had said.

The nursery was silent. It was empty as a jungle glade at hot high noon. The walls were blank and two dimensional. Now, as George and Lydia Hadley stood in the center of the room, the walls began to purr and recede into crystalline distance, it seemed, and presently an African veldt appeared, in three dimensions; on all sides, in colors reproduced to the final pebble and bit of straw. The ceiling above them became a deep sky with a hot yellow sun.

George Hadley felt the perspiration start on his brow.

"Let's get out of the sun," he said. "This is a little too real. But I don't see anything wrong."

"Wait a moment, you'll see," said his wife.

Now the hidden odorophonics were beginning to blow a wind of odor at the two people in the middle of the baked veldtland. The hot straw smell of lion grass, the cool green smell of the hidden water hole, the great rusty smell of animals, the smell of dust like a red paprika in the hot air. And now the sounds: the thump of distant antelope feet on sod, the papery rustling of vultures. A shadow passed through the sky. The shadow flickered on George Hadley's upturned, sweating face.

"Filthy creatures," he heard his wife say.

"The vultures."

• *veldt* high flat land in southern Africa that is covered in grass and has few trees
1 *nursery* (old-fashioned) a room in a house where children play
15 *rock sb.* jdn. schaukeln
16 *sensitize sth.* make sth. react due to a physical or chemical signal
21 *thatched* aus Stroh oder Reet gemacht
25 *glade* (fml) a small open area in a forest
27 *purr* make a low cat-like sound
27 *recede* move gradually away (into the distance)
28 *crystalline* (fml) very clear like crystals
30 *pebble* Kieselstein
36 *odorophonics* (here) equipment producing smell and sounds
38 *lion grass* type of tall grass
40 *thump* sound of sth. hitting the ground hard
40 *sod* (fml) (Gras)sode
41 *papery* thin and dry like paper
41 *rustling* sound of light things (e.g. leaves) moving together
41 *vulture* bird that eats the flesh of dead animals
42 *flicker* appear for a short time

"You see, there are the lions, far over, that way. Now they're on their way to the water hole. They've just been eating," said Lydia. "I don't know what."

"Some animal." George Hadley put his hand up to shield off the burning light from his squinted eyes. "A zebra or a baby giraffe, maybe."

"Are you sure?" His wife sounded peculiarly tense.

"No, it's a little late to be *sure*," he said, amused. "Nothing over there I can see but cleaned bone, and the vultures dropping for what's left."

"Did you hear that scream?" she asked.

"No."

"About a minute ago?"

"Sorry, no."

The lions were coming. And again George Hadley was filled with admiration for the mechanical genius who had conceived this room. A miracle of efficiency selling for an absurdly low price. Every home should have one. Oh, occasionally they frightened you with their clinical accuracy, they startled you, gave you a twinge, but most of the time what fun for everyone, not only your own son and daughter, but for yourself when you felt like a quick jaunt to a foreign land, a quick change of scenery. Well, here it was!

And here were the lions now, fifteen feet away, so real, so feverishly and startlingly real that you could feel the prickling fur on your hand, and your mouth was stuffed with the dusty upholstery smell of their heated pelts, and the yellow of them was in your eyes like the yellow of an exquisite French tapestry, the yellows of lions and summer grass, and the sound of the matted lion lungs exhaling on the silent noontide, and the smell of meat from the panting, dripping mouths.

The lions stood looking at George and Lydia Hadley with terrible green-yellow eyes.

"Watch out!" screamed Lydia.

The lions came running at them.

Lydia bolted and ran. Instinctively, George sprang after her. Outside, in the hall, with the door slammed, he was laughing and she was crying, and they both stood appalled at the other's reaction.

"George!"

"Lydia! Oh, my dear poor sweet Lydia!"

"They almost got us!"

"Walls, Lydia, remember; crystal walls, that's all they are. Oh, they look real, I must admit – Africa in your parlor – but it's all dimensional superreactionary, supersensitive color film and mental tape film behind glass screens. It's all odorophonics and sonics, Lydia. Here's my handkerchief."

"I'm afraid." She came to him and put her body against him and cried steadily. "Did you see? Did you *feel*? It's too real."

"Now, Lydia ..."

49 *squint* zusammenkneifen
59 *conceive sth.* develop an idea of or plan for sth.
62 *startle sb.* surprise sb. suddenly
62 *twinge* sudden short feeling of pain
64 *jaunt* short pleasure trip
67 *prickle* cause an unpleasant sensation on the skin
67 *fur* Fell
68 *upholstery* soft covering on armchairs and sofas; (here) skin and fur of the animals
69 *pelt* skin with fur or hair on animals
70 *tapestry* Bildteppich
71 *matted* verfilzt, belegt
71 *exhale* breathe out
71 *noontide* (fml) around 12 o'clock in the middle of the day
72 *pant* breathe quickly with short breaths
72 *drip* produce drops of liquid
77 *bolt* run away suddenly and frightened
85 *superreactionary* (hier) schnell reagierend und sehr farbecht
86 *sonics* (here) method of producing sound
89 *steady* not changing

"You've got to tell Wendy and Peter not to read any more on Africa."

"Of course – of course." He patted her.

"Promise?"

"Sure."

"And lock the nursery for a few days until I get my nerves settled."

"You know how difficult Peter is about that. When I punished him a month ago by locking the nursery for even a few hours – the tantrum he threw! And Wendy too. They *live* for the nursery."

"It's got to be locked, that's all there is to it."

"All right." Reluctantly he locked the huge door. "You've been working too hard. You need a rest."

"I don't know – I don't know," she said, blowing her nose, sitting down in a chair that immediately began to rock and comfort her. "Maybe I don't have enough to do. Maybe I have time to think too much. Why don't we shut the whole house off for a few days and take a vacation?"

"You mean you want to fry my eggs for me?"

"Yes." She nodded.

"And darn my socks?"

"Yes." A frantic, watery-eyed nodding.

"And sweep the house?"

"Yes, yes – oh, yes!"

"But I thought that's why we bought this house, so we wouldn't have to do anything?"

"That's just it. I feel like I don't belong here. The house is wife and mother now and nursemaid. Can I compete with an African veldt? Can I give a bath and scrub the children as efficiently or quickly as the automatic scrub bath can? I can not. And it isn't just me. It's you. You've been awfully nervous lately."

"I suppose I have been smoking too much."

"You look as if you didn't know what to do with yourself in this house, either. You smoke a little more every morning and drink a little more every afternoon and need a little more sedative every night. You're beginning to feel unnecessary too."

"Am I?" He paused and tried to feel into himself to see what was really there.

"Oh, George!" She looked beyond him, at the nursery door. "Those lions can't get out of there, can they?"

He looked at the door and saw it tremble as if something had jumped against it from the other side.

"Of course not," he said.

At dinner they ate alone, for Wendy and Peter were at a special plastic carnival across town and had televised home to say they'd be late, to go ahead eating. So George Hadley, bemused, sat watching the dining-room table produce warm dishes of food from its mechanical interior.

"We forgot the ketchup," he said.

93 *pat sb.* jdn. tätscheln
96 *settled* calm
98 *tantrum* an outburst of angry, unreasonable behaviour, esp. by children
101 *reluctant* hesitating
109 *darn sth.* etwas stopfen
110 *frantic* unable to control your emotions; extremely worried
110 *watery-eyed* tränenfeucht
116 *nursemaid* (old-fashioned) woman who looks after a family's children
117 *scrub sb.* jdn. schrubben
123 *sedative* drug which calms you down
133 *televise* (here) send a message via videophone
133–134 *go ahead doing sth.* do sth. without sb.
134 *bemused* confused, bewildered

"Sorry," said a small voice within the table, and ketchup appeared.

'INTELLIGENT' FURNITURE

As for the nursery, thought George Hadley, it won't hurt for the children to be locked out of it awhile. Too much of anything isn't good for anyone. And it was clearly indicated that the children had been spending a little too much time on Africa. That *sun*. He could feel it on his neck, still, like a hot paw. And the *lions*. And the smell of blood. Remarkable how the nursery caught the telepathic emanations of the children's minds and created life to fill their every desire. The children thought lions, and there were lions. The children thought zebras, and there were zebras. Sun – sun. Giraffes – giraffes. Death and death.

TELEPATHIC, MIND-READING SYSTEMS

That *last*. He chewed tastelessly on the meat that the table had cut for him. Death thoughts. They were awfully young, Wendy and Peter, for death thoughts. Or, no, you were never too young, really. Long before you knew what death was you were wishing it on someone else. When you were two years old you were shooting people with cap pistols.

But this – the long, hot African veldt – the awful death in the jaws of a lion. And repeated again and again.

"Where are you going?"

He didn't answer Lydia. Preoccupied, he let the lights glow softly on ahead of him, extinguish behind him as he padded to the nursery door. He listened against it. Far away, a lion roared.

He unlocked the door and opened it. Just before he stepped inside, he heard a faraway scream. And then another roar from the lions, which subsided quickly.

He stepped into Africa. How many times in the last year had he opened this door and found Wonderland, Alice, the Mock Turtle, or Aladdin and his Magical Lamp, or Jack Pumpkinhead of Oz, or Dr. Doolittle, or the cow jumping over a very real-appearing moon – all the delightful contraptions of a make-believe world. How often had he seen Pegasus flying in the sky ceiling, or seen fountains of red fireworks, or heard angel voices singing. But now, this yellow hot Africa, this bake oven with murder in the heat. Perhaps Lydia was right. Perhaps they needed a little vacation from the fantasy which was growing a bit too real for ten-year-old children. It was all right to exercise one's mind with gymnastic fantasies, but when the lively child mind settled on *one* pattern ...? It seemed that, at a distance, for the past month, he had heard lions roaring, and smelled their strong odor seeping as far away as his study door. But, being busy, he had paid it no attention.

George Hadley stood on the African grassland alone. The lions looked up from their feeding, watching him. The only flaw to the illusion was the open door through which he could see his wife, far down the dark hall, like a framed picture, eating her dinner abstractedly.

"Go away," he said to the lions.

They did not go.

He knew the principle of the room exactly. You sent out your thoughts. Whatever you thought would appear. "Let's have Aladdin and his lamp," he snapped.

143 *telepathic* being able to communicate only from mind to mind
143 *emanation* Ausstrahlen, Ausströmen
151 *cap pistol* Platzpatronengewehr, Spielzeuggewehr
155 *preoccupied* thinking or worrying about sth.
156 *pad* (here) walk with soft steps
160 *subside* become quieter
162 *Wonderland, Alice, Mock Turtle* references to Lewis Caroll's novel *Alice's Adventures in Wonderland* (1865)
163 *Aladdin and the Magical Lamp* famous tale from *One Thousand and One Nights*
163 *Jack Pumpkinhead, Oz* reference to a character of the famous Oz children novels by L. Frank Baum
164 *Dr. Doolittle* doctor in Hugh Lofting's series of children's novels who is able to talk to animals
165 *contraption* strange-looking machine
165 *make-believe world* world of fantasy
166 *Pegasus* winged horse from Greek mythology
171 *gymnastic* turnerisch
173 *seep* (of a liquid or gas) flow slowly
176 *flaw* fault
178 *abstracted* (fml) geistesabwesend
183 *snap* say quickly and determinedly

The veldtland remained; the lions remained.

"Come on, room, I demand Aladdin!" he said.

Nothing happened. The lions mumbled in their baked pelts.

"Aladdin!"

He went back to dinner. "The fool room's out of order," he said. "It won't respond."

"Or –"

"Or what?"

"Or it *can't* respond," said Lydia, "because the children have thought about Africa and lions and killing so many days that the room's in a rut."

Personification

"Could be."

"Or Peter's set it to remain that way."

"Set it?"

"He may have got into the machinery and fixed something."

"Peter doesn't know machinery."

"He's a wise one for ten. That I.Q. of his –"

"Nevertheless –"

"Hello, Mom. Hello, Dad."

The Hadleys turned. Wendy and Peter were coming in the front door, cheeks like peppermint candy, eyes like bright blue agate marbles, a smell of ozone on their jumpers from their trip in the helicopter.

AIR TRAVEL AS NORMALITY

"You're just in time for supper," said both parents.

"We're full of strawberry ice cream and hot dogs," said the children, holding hands. "But we'll sit and watch."

"Yes, come tell us about the nursery," said George Hadley.

The brother and sister blinked at him and then at each other. "Nursery?"

"All about Africa and everything," said the father with false joviality.

"I don't understand," said Peter.

"Your mother and I were just traveling through Africa with rod and reel; Tom Swift and his Electric Lion," said George Hadley.

"There's no Africa in the nursery," said Peter simply.

"Oh, come now, Peter. We know better."

"I don't remember any Africa," said Peter to Wendy. "Do you?"

"No"

"Run see and come tell."

She obeyed.

"Wendy, come back here!" said George Hadley, but she was gone. The house lights followed her like a flock of fireflies. Too late, he realized he had forgotten to lock the nursery door after his last inspection.

"Wendy'll look and come tell us," said Peter.

"She doesn't have to tell *me*. I've seen it."

"I'm sure you're mistaken, Father."

"I'm not, Peter. Come along now,"

But Wendy was back. "It's not Africa," she said breathlessly.

193–194 *the room's in a rut* der Raum steckt in einem bestimmten Trott
204 *agate* Achat
204 *marble* a small ball of colored glass children play with
210 *blink* shut and open your eyes very quickly
212 *joviality* friendliness, cheerfulness
219–220 *rod and reel* (hier) Angelrute
220 *Tom Swift and his Electric Lion* reference to an American series of juvenile adventure stories, one of which was entitled *Tom Swift and His Electric Rifle* (1911)
228 *flock* large group of animals
228 *firefly* a flying insect with a tail that shines in the dark

"We'll see about this," said George Hadley, and they all walked down the hall together and opened the nursery door.

There was a green, lovely forest, a lovely river, a purple mountain, high voices singing, and Rima, lovely and mysterious, lurking in the trees with colorful flights of butterflies, like animated bouquets, lingering in her long hair. The African veldtland was gone. The lions were gone. Only Rima was here now, singing a song so beautiful that it brought tears to your eyes.

George Hadley looked in at the changed scene. "Go to bed," he said to the children.

They opened their mouths.

"You heard me," he said.

They went off to the air closet, where a wind sucked them like brown leaves up the flue to their slumber rooms.

REVOLUTIONARY ELEVATORS, "LETTER CHUTE"

George Hadley walked through the singing glade and picked up something that lay in the corner near where the lions had been. He walked slowly back to his wife.

"What is that?" she asked.

"An old wallet of mine," he said.

He showed it to her. The smell of hot grass was on it and the smell of a lion. There were drops of saliva on it, it had been chewed, and there were blood smears on both sides.

He closed the nursery door and locked it, tight.

In the middle of the night he was still awake and he knew his wife was awake. "Do you think Wendy changed it?" she said at last, in the dark room.

DISTRUST

"Of course."

"Made it from a veldt into a forest and put Rima there instead of lions?"

"Yes."

"Why?"

"I don't know. But it's staying locked until I find out."

"How did your wallet get there?"

"I don't know anything," he said, "except that I'm beginning to be sorry we bought that room for the children. If children are neurotic at all, a room like that –"

"It's supposed to help them work off their neuroses in a healthful way."

"I'm starting to wonder." He stared at the ceiling.

"We've given the children everything they ever wanted. Is this our reward – secrecy, disobedience?"

"Who was it said, 'Children are carpets, they should be stepped on occasionally'? We've never lifted a hand. They're insufferable – let's admit it. They come and go when they like, they treat us as if we were offspring. They're spoiled and we're spoiled."

"They've been acting funny ever since you forbade them to take the rocket to New York a few months ago."

238 *Rima* young woman female protagonist of William Henry Hudson's exotic romance, *Green Mansions: A Romance of the Tropical Forest* (1904)
238 *lurk* lauern
239 *animated* appearing as if moving
239 *bouquet* bunch of arranged flowers
239 *linger* verweilen
248 *flue* (hier) Luftstromrohr
248 *slumber room* (here) bedroom
255 *saliva* [sə'laɪvə] liquid produced in the mouth to help swallow food
256 *smear* Fleck
275 *secrecy* ['siːkrəsi] Heimlichtuerei
275 *disobedience* refusal to obey
279 *offspring* children
279 *spoiled* (adj) verwöhnt

"They're not old enough to do that alone, I explained."

"Nevertheless, I've noticed they've been decidedly cool toward us since."

"I think I'll have David McClean come tomorrow morning to have a look at Africa."

"But it's not Africa now, it's Green Mansions country and Rima."

"I have a feeling it'll be Africa again before then."

A moment later they heard the screams.

Two screams. Two people screaming from downstairs. And then a roar of lions.

"Wendy and Peter aren't in their rooms," said his wife.

He lay in his bed with his beating heart. "No," he said. "They've broken into the nursery."

"Those screams – they sound familiar."

"Do they?"

"Yes, awfully."

And although their beds tried very hard, the two adults couldn't be rocked to sleep for another hour. A smell of cats was in the night air.

"Father?" said Peter.

"Yes."

Peter looked at his shoes. He never looked at his father any more, nor at his mother. "You aren't going to lock up the nursery for good, are you?"

"That all depends."

"On what?" snapped Peter.

"On you and your sister. If you intersperse this Africa with a little variety – oh, Sweden perhaps, or Denmark or China –"

"I thought we were free to play as we wished."

"You are, within reasonable bounds."

"What's wrong with Africa, Father?"

"Oh, so now you admit you have been conjuring up Africa, do you?"

"I wouldn't want the nursery locked up," said Peter coldly. "Ever."

"Matter of fact, we're thinking of turning the whole house off for about a month. Live sort of a carefree one-for-all existence."

"That sounds dreadful! Would I have to tie my own shoes instead of letting the shoe tier do it? And brush my own teeth and comb my hair and give myself a bath?"

"It would be fun for a change, don't you think?"

"No, it would be horrid. I didn't like it when you took out the picture painter last month."

"That's because I wanted you to learn to paint all by yourself, son."

"I don't want to do anything but look and listen and smell; what else is there to do?"

"All right, go play in Africa."

"Will you shut off the house sometime soon?"

283 *decidedly* definitely and in an obvious way
303 *for good* for ever
307 *intersperse* einstreuen
310 *bounds* (pl) limits
312 *conjure sth. up* create sth., evoke a picture of sth. in your mind
316 *one for all* everyone being there to help everyone else
321 *horrid* terrible

"We're considering it."

"I don't think you'd better consider it any more, Father."

"I won't have any threats from my son!"

"Very well." And Peter strolled off to the nursery.

"Am I on time?" said David McClean.

"Breakfast?" asked George Hadley.

"Thanks, had some. What's the trouble?"

"David, you're a psychologist."

"I should hope so."

"Well, then, have a look at our nursery. You saw it a year ago when you dropped by; did you notice anything peculiar about it then?"

"Can't say I did; the usual violences, a tendency toward a slight paranoia here or there, usual in children because they feel persecuted by parents constantly, but, oh, really nothing."

They walked down the hall. "I locked the nursery up," explained the father, "and the children broke back into it during the night. I let them stay so they could form the patterns for you to see."

There was a terrible screaming from the nursery.

"There it is," said George Hadley. "See what you make of it."

They walked in on the children without rapping.

The screams had faded. The lions were feeding.

"Run outside a moment, children," said George Hadley. "No, don't change the mental combination. Leave the walls as they are. Get!"

With the children gone, the two men stood studying the lions clustered at a distance, eating with great relish whatever it was they had caught.

"I wish I knew what it was," said George Hadley. "Sometimes I can almost see. Do you think if I brought high-powered binoculars here and –"

David McClean laughed dryly. "Hardly." He turned to study all four walls. "How long has this been going on?"

"A little over a month."

"It certainly doesn't *feel* good."

"I want facts, not feelings."

"My dear George, a psychologist never saw a fact in his life. He only hears about feelings; vague things. This doesn't feel good, I tell you. Trust my hunches and my instincts. I have a nose for something bad. This is very bad. My advice to you is to have the whole damn room torn down and your children brought to me every day during the next year for treatment."

"Is that that bad?"

"I'm afraid so. One of the original uses of these nurseries was so that we could study the patterns left on the walls by the child's mind, study at our leisure, and help the child. In this case, however, the room has become a channel toward – destructive thoughts, instead of a release away from them."

331 *stroll* walk slowly and casually
338 *drop by* visit sb.
340 *paranoia* mental state which causes people to have unreasonable fears about others
347 *rap* knock
350 *get!* (here) go
352 *cluster* come together in a small group
352 *relish* great enjoyment or pleasure
364 *hunch* intuitive feeling that sth. is true although there is not any evidence
372 *release* act of freeing sb.

"Didn't you sense this before?"

"I sensed only that you had spoiled your children more than most. And now you're letting them down in some way. What way?"

"I wouldn't let them go to New York."

"What else?"

"I've taken a few machines from the house and threatened them, a month ago, with closing up the nursery unless they did their homework. I did close it for a few days to show I meant business."

"Ah, ha!"

"Does that mean anything?"

"Everything. Where before they had a Santa Claus now they have a Scrooge. Children prefer Santas. You've let this room and this house replace you and your wife in your children's affections. This room is their mother and father, far more important in their lives than their real parents. And now you come along and want to shut it off. No wonder there's hatred here. You can feel it coming out of the sky. Feel that sun. George, you'll have to change your life. Like too many others, you've built it around creature comforts. Why, you'd starve tomorrow if something went wrong in your kitchen. You wouldn't know how to tap an egg. Nevertheless, turn everything off. Start new. It'll take time. But we'll make good children out of bad in a year, wait and see."

"But won't the shock be too much for the children, shutting the room up abruptly, for good?"

"I don't want them going any deeper into this, that's all." The lions were finished with their red feast.

The lions were standing on the edge of the clearing watching the two men.

"Now *I'm* feeling persecuted," said McClean. "Let's get out of here. I never have cared for these damned rooms. Make me nervous."

"The lions look real, don't they?" said George Hadley. "I don't suppose there's any way –"

"What?"

"– that they could *become* real?"

"Not that I know."

"Some flaw in the machinery, a tampering or something?"

"No."

The went to the door.

"I don't imagine the room will like being turned off," said the father.

"Nothing ever likes to die – even a room."

"I wonder if it hates me for wanting to switch it off?"

"Paranoia is thick around here today," said David McClean. "You can follow it like a spoor. Hello." He bent and picked up a bloody scarf. "This yours?"

"No." George Hadley's face was rigid. "It belongs to Lydia."

They went to the fuse box together and threw the switch that killed the nursery.

385 *Scrooge* a character in Charles Dickens's *A Christmas Carol* who is very mean
386 *affection* the feeling of liking or loving sb./sth.
391 *creature comforts* (pl) all the things that make life pleasant
392 *tap an egg* ein Ei aufschlagen
408 *tampering* Herumpfuschen
416 *spoor* a track or smell left by animals

The two children were in hysterics. They screamed and pranced and threw things. They yelled and sobbed and swore and jumped at the furniture.

"You can't do that to the nursery, you can't!"

"Now, children."

The children flung themselves onto a couch, weeping.

"George," said Lydia Hadley, "turn on the nursery, just for a few moments. You can't be so abrupt."

"No."

"You can't be so cruel."

"Lydia, it's off, and it stays off. And the whole damn house dies as of here and now. The more I see of the mess we've put ourselves in, the more it sickens me. We've been contemplating our mechanical, electronic navels for too long. My God, how we need a breath of honest air!"

And he marched about the house turning off the voice clocks, the stoves, the heaters, the shoe shiners, the shoe lacers, the body scrubbers and swabbers and massagers, and every other machine he could put his hand to.

The house was full of dead bodies, it seemed. It felt like a mechanical cemetery. So silent. None of the humming hidden energy of machines waiting to function at the tap of a button.

"Don't let them do it!" wailed Peter at the ceiling, as if he was talking to the house, the nursery. "Don't let Father kill everything." He turned to his father. "Oh, I hate you!"

"Insults won't get you anywhere."

"I wish you were dead!"

"We were, for a long while. Now we're going to really start living. Instead of being handled and massaged, we're going to *live*."

Wendy was still crying and Peter joined her again. "Just a moment, just one moment, just another moment of nursery," they wailed.

"Oh, George," said the wife, "it can't hurt."

"All right – all right, if they'll only just shut up. One minute, mind you, and then off forever."

"Daddy, Daddy, Daddy!" sang the children, smiling with wet faces.

"And then we're going on a vacation. David McClean is coming back in half an hour to help us move out and get to the airport. I'm going to dress. You turn the nursery on for a minute, Lydia, just a minute, mind you."

And the three of them went babbling off while he let himself be vacuumed upstairs through the air flue and set about dressing himself. A minute later Lydia appeared.

"I'll be glad when we get away," she sighed.

"Did you leave them in the nursery?"

"I wanted to dress too. Oh, that horrid Africa. What can they see in it?"

"Well, in five minutes we'll be on our way to Iowa. Lord, how did we ever get in this house? What prompted us to buy a nightmare?"

421 *prance* (hier) herumaufstapfen
433–434 *contemplate your navel* think about yourself too much and not about more important things
437 *swabber* (hier) Maschine, die wischt
459 *babble* talk quickly and excitedly
460 *vacuum sb.* (hier) move sb. by the force of a vacuum
467 *prompt sb. to do sth.* make sb. do sth. in the first place

"Pride, money, foolishness."

"I think we'd better get downstairs before those kids get engrossed with those damned beasts again."

Just then they heard the children calling, "Daddy, Mommy, come quick – quick!"

They went downstairs in the air flue and ran down the hall.

The children were nowhere in sight. "Wendy? Peter!"

They ran into the nursery. The veldtland was empty save for the lions waiting, looking at them. "Peter, Wendy?"

The door slammed.

"Wendy, Peter!"

George Hadley and his wife whirled and ran back to the door.

"Open the door!" cried George Hadley, trying the knob. "Why, they've locked it from the outside! Peter!" He beat at the door. "Open up!"

He heard Peter's voice outside, against the door.

"Don't let them switch off the nursery and the house," he was saying.

Mr. and Mrs. George Hadley beat at the door. "Now, don't be ridiculous, children. It's time to go. Mr. McClean'll be here in a minute and ..."

And then they heard the sounds.

The lions on three sides of them, in the yellow veldt grass, padding through the dry straw, rumbling and roaring in their throats.

The lions.

Mr. Hadley looked at his wife and they turned and looked back at the beasts edging slowly forward, crouching, tails stiff.

Mr. and Mrs. Hadley screamed.

And suddenly they realized why those other screams had sounded familiar.

"Well, here I am," said David McClean in the nursery doorway. "Oh, hello." He stared at the two children seated in the center of the open glade eating a little picnic lunch. Beyond them was the water hole and the yellow veldtland; above was the hot sun. He began to perspire. "Where are your father and mother?"

The children looked up and smiled. "Oh, they'll be here directly."

"Good, we must get going." At a distance Mr. McClean saw the lions fighting and clawing and then quieting down to feed in silence under the shady trees.

He squinted at the lions with his hand up to his eyes.

Now the lions were done feeding. They moved to the water hole to drink.

A shadow flickered over Mr. McClean's hot face. Many shadows flickered. The vultures were dropping down the blazing sky.

"A cup of tea?" asked Wendy in the silence.

469–470 *engrossed with sth.* so interested in sth. that you give it all your attention
479 *whirl* (here) turn around quickly
491 *rumble* make long deep sounds
494 *edge* move slowly and carefully
494 *crouch* kauern
507 *squint at sth.* look at sth. with your eyes partly closed so that you can see better
511 *blazing* (adj) extremely hot

Assignments

1 Summarize the plot of the story.

2 a) List all the amenities the "Happy-life Home" seems to offer and describe the impact on the characters' lives.
b) Compare the gadgets mentioned in the story to the state of the art of modern home technology available in our lives.

3 Examine the language used for and in relation with the technological equipment of the house.

4 a) Focus on the "nursery": Describe its function, the way it works, its effects, and its impact on the family.
b) Discuss whether the "nursery" and its consequences can be applied to issues of young people's media usage today.

5 a) Analyze the point of view of the story.
b) Rewrite a selected passage of the story from one of the character's point of view (1st person singular) or from alternating perspectives.

6 Describe the parent-child relationship as it is depicted by the author.

7 Outline the psychologist's advice and comment on it.

8 Interpret the statistical material below on parental worries concerning their children's use of the media and relate it to "The Veldt".

Chart 1

Percent of parents who say they are most concerned about inappropriate content in:

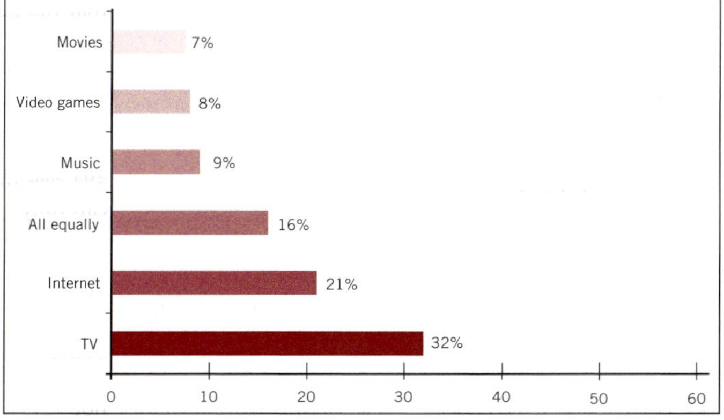

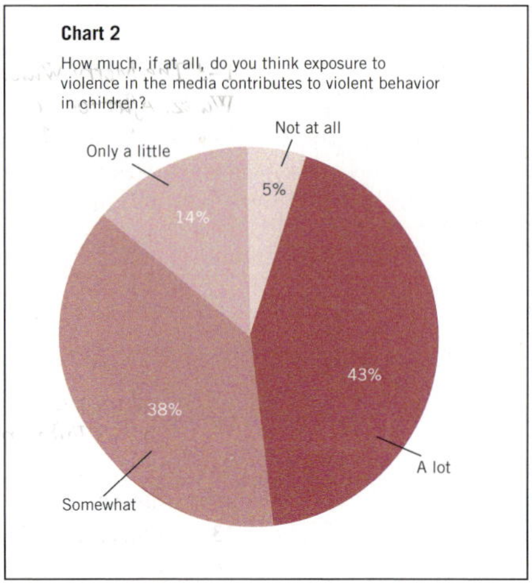

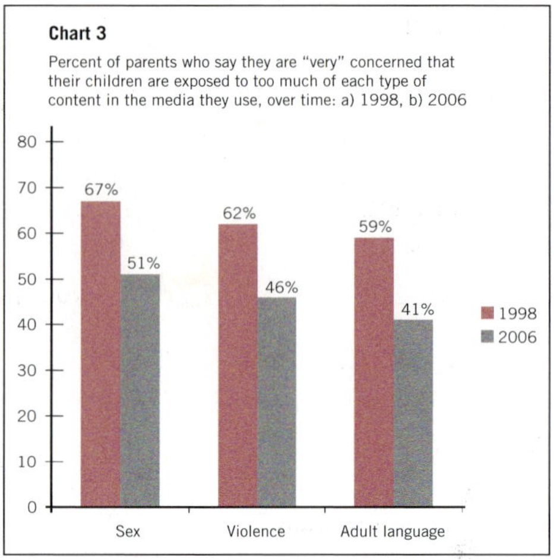

Source: *Parents,* ***Children & Media: A Kaiser Family Foundation Survey*** *(June, 2007). http://www.kff.org/entmedia/upload/7638.pdf*

9 Interpret this cartoon and relate it to Bradbury's story "The Veldt".

From: *Bob Englehart, "Computer Time", in:* ***The Hartford Courant,*** *18 January 2005*

10 Formulate educational guidelines for parents of our modern technological age.

The Murderer

Music moved with him in the white halls. He passed an office door: "The Merry Widow Waltz." Another door: "Afternoon of a Faun." A third: "Kiss Me Again." He turned into a cross corridor: "The Sword Dance" buried him in cymbals, drums, pots, pans, knives, forks, thunder, and tin lightning. All washed away as he hurried through an ante-room where a secretary sat nicely stunned by Beethoven's Fifth. He moved himself before her eyes like a hand; she didn't see him.

His wrist radio buzzed.

"Yes?"

"This is Lee, Dad. Don't forget about my allowance."

"Yes, son, yes. I'm busy."

"Just didn't want you to forget, Dad," said the wrist radio. Tchaikovsky's "Romeo and Juliet" swarmed about the voice and flushed into the long halls.

The psychiatrist moved in the beehive of offices, in the cross-pollination of themes, Stravinsky mating with Bach, Haydn unsuccessfully repulsing Rachmaninoff, Schubert slain by Duke Ellington. He nodded to the humming secretaries and the whistling doctors fresh to their morning work. At his office he checked a few papers with his stenographer, who sang under her breath, then phoned the police captain upstairs. A few minutes later a red light blinked, a voice said from the ceiling:

"Prisoner delivered to Interview Chamber Nine."

He unlocked the chamber door, stepped in, heard the door lock behind him.

"Go away," said the prisoner, smiling.

The psychiatrist was shocked by that smile. A very sunny, pleasant warm thing, a thing that shed bright light upon the room. Dawn among the dark hills. High noon at midnight, that smile. The blue eyes sparkled serenely above that display of self-assured dentistry.

"I'm here to help you," said the psychiatrist, frowning. Something was wrong with the room. He had hesitated the moment he entered. He glanced around. The prisoner laughed. "If you're wondering why it's so quiet in here, I just kicked the radio to death."

Violent, thought the doctor.

The prisoner read this thought, smiled, put out a gentle hand. "No, only to machines that yak-yak-yak."

Bits of the wall radio's tubes and wires lay on the gray carpeting. Ignoring these, feeling that smile upon him like a heat lamp, the psychiatrist sat across from his patient in the unusual silence which was like the gathering of a storm.

"You're Mr. Albert Brock, who calls himself The Murderer?"

Brock nodded pleasantly. "Before we start ..." He moved quietly and quickly to detach the wrist radio from the doctor's arm. He tucked it in his teeth like a walnut, gritted and heard it crack, handed it back to the

1–3 *The Merry Widow Waltz, Afternoon of a Faun, Kiss Me Again, The Sword Dance* various songs and pieces of music
4 *cymbal* (Schlaginstrument) Becken
4–5 *tin lightning* Blechgewitter
5 *ante-room* Vorzimmer
6 *stunned* impressed
6 *Beethoven's Fifth* one of Beethoven's nine symphonies
13 *Tchaikovsky's "Romeo and Juliet"* musical work inspired by Shakespeare's play
13 *swarm* move around in large groups (like insects)
13 *flush* suddenly flow
15 *beehive* Bienenstock
15–16 *cross-pollination* Fremdbestäubung
16 *mate* have sex in order to have children
17 *repulse sb.* drive sb. away
17 *slay sb. (slain – slain)* kill sb.
18 *hum* summen
18 *whistle* pfeifen
18 *fresh (here)* recently arrive
19 *stenographer* (old-fashioned) Schreibkraft
27 *shed sth.* (hier) etwas verbreiten
28 *sparkle* shine brightly with flashes of light
29 *serene* peaceful and relaxed
29 *self-assured* self-confident
29 *dentistry* (here) mouth and teeth
30 *frown* die Stirn runzeln
32 *glance around* look quickly around
40 *gathering* (n) Heraufziehen
43 *detach sth.* remove sth. from sth. else
43 *tuck sth.* etwas stecken
44 *grit sth.* grind sth. with your teeth

appalled psychiatrist as if he had done them both a favor. “That's better.”

The psychiatrist stared at the ruined machine. “You're running up quite a damage bill.”

“I don't care,” smiled the patient. “As the old song goes: ‘Don't Care What Happens to Me!’ ” He hummed it.

The psychiatrist said: “Shall we start?”

“Fine. The first victim, or one of the first, was my telephone. Murder most foul. I shoved it in the kitchen Insinkerator! Stopped the disposal unit in mid-swallow. Poor thing strangled to death. After that I shot the television set!”

The psychiatrist said, “Mmm.”

“Fired six shots right through the cathode. Made a beautiful tinkling crash, like a dropped chandelier.”

“Nice imagery.”

“Thanks, I always dreamt of being a writer.”

“Suppose you tell me when you first began to hate the telephone.”

“It frightened me as a child. Uncle of mine called it the Ghost Machine. Voices without bodies. Scared the living hell out of me. Later in life I was never comfortable. Seemed to me a phone was an impersonal instrument. If it *felt* like it, it let your personality go through its wires. If it didn't *want* to, it just drained your personality away until what slipped through at the other end was some cold fish of a voice all steel, copper, plastic, no warmth, no reality. It's easy to say the wrong thing on telephones; the telephone changes your meaning on you. First thing you know, you've made an enemy. Then, of course, the telephone's such a *convenient* thing; it just sits there and *demands* you call someone who doesn't want to be called. Friends were always calling, calling, calling me. Hell, I hadn't any time of my own. When it wasn't the telephone it was the television, the radio, the phonograph. When it wasn't the television or radio or the phonograph it was motion pictures at the corner theater, motion pictures projected, with commercials on low-lying cumulus clouds. It doesn't rain rain any more, it rains soapsuds. When it wasn't High-Fly Cloud advertisements, it was music by Mozzek in every restaurant; music and commercials on the busses I rode to work. When it wasn't music, it was interoffice communications, and my horror chamber of a radio wrist watch on which my friends and my wife phoned every five minutes. What is there about such ‘conveniences’ that makes them so *temptingly* convenient? The average man thinks, Here I am, time on my hands, and there on my wrist is a wrist telephone, so why not just buzz old Joe up, eh? ‘Hello, hello!’ I love my friends, my wife, humanity, very much, but when one minute my wife calls to say, ‘Where are you *now*, dear?’ and a friend calls and says, ‘Got the best off-color joke to tell you. Seems there was a guy –’ And a stranger calls and cries out, ‘This is the Find-Fax Poll. What gum are you chewing at this very *instant*!’ Well!”

“How did you feel during the week?”

45 *appalled* [ə'pɔːld] feeling horror
47–48 *run up a bill* allow yourself to owe more and more money
52–53 *murder most foul* quote from Shakespeare's *Hamlet* (I, v, 27–28),
53 *Insinkerator* (here) futuristic kitchen garbage disposal
57 *cathode* Katodenstrahlröhre
58 *chandelier* Kronleuchter
63 *scare the living hell out of sb.* (infml) make sb. very frightened
66 *drain sth. away* make sth. flow away
74 *phonograph* (old-fashioned) record player
75 *motion picture* (AE, old fashioned) film made for the cinema
77 *soapsuds* (pl) Seifenblasen
78 *Mozzek* allusion to the company Muzak, which devloped background music played in shops, elevators, etc.
82 *convenience* gadget that makes life easier and more comfortable
83 *convenient* easy, quick and comfortable
85 *buzz sb. up* (infml AE) jdn. anrufen
87 *off-color joke* (AE) indecent joke, usu. relating to sex

"The fuse lit. On the edge of the cliff. That same afternoon I did what I did at the office."

"Which was?"

"I poured a paper cup of water into the intercommunications system."

The psychiatrist wrote on his pad.

"And the system shorted?"

"Beautifully! The Fourth of July on wheels! My God, stenographers ran around looking *lost*! What an uproar!"

"Felt better temporarily, eh?"

"Fine! Then I got the idea at noon of stomping my wrist radio on the sidewalk. A shrill voice was just yelling out of it at me, 'This is People's Poll Number Nine. What did you eat for lunch?' when I kicked the Jesus out of the wrist radio!"

"Felt even *better*, eh?"

"It *grew* on me!" Brock rubbed his hands together. "Why didn't I start a solitary revolution, deliver man from certain 'conveniences'? 'Convenient for whom?' I cried. Convenient for friends: 'Hey, Al, thought I'd call you from the locker room out here at Green Hills. Just made a sockdolager hole in one! A hole in one, Al! A *beautiful* day. Having a shot of whiskey now. Thought you'd want to know, Al!' Convenient for my office, so when I'm in the field with my radio car there's no moment when I'm not in touch. In *touch*! *There's* a slimy phrase. Touch, hell. *Gripped*! Pawed, rather. Mauled and massaged and pounded by FM voices. You can't leave your car without checking in: 'Have stopped to visit gas-station men's room.' 'Okay, Brock, step on it!' 'Brock, what *took* you so long?' 'Sorry, sir.' 'Watch it next time, Brock.' *'Yes, sir!'* So, do you know what I did, Doctor? I bought a quart of French chocolate ice cream and spooned it into the car radio transmitter."

"Was there any *special* reason for selecting French chocolate ice cream to spoon into the broadcasting unit?"

Brock thought about it and smiled. "It's my favorite flavor."

"Oh," said the doctor.

"I figured, hell, what's good enough for me is good enough for the radio transmitter."

"What made you think of spooning *ice cream* into the radio?"

"It was a hot day."

The doctor paused.

"And what happened next?"

"Silence happened next. God, it was *beautiful*. That car radio cackling all day, Brock go here, Brock go there, Brock check in, Brock check out, okay Brock, hour lunch, Brock, lunch over, Brock, Brock, Brock. Well, that silence was like putting ice cream in my ears."

"You seem to like ice cream a lot."

"I just rode around feeling of the silence. It's a big bolt of the nicest, softest flannel ever made. Silence. A whole hour of it. I just sat in my car; smiling, feeling of that flannel with my ears. I felt *drunk* with Freedom!"

97 *short* (v, infml) = *short-circuit* ['sɜːrkɪt] an einem Kurzschluss zusammenbrechen
98 *The Fourth of July on wheels* (etwa:) welch herrliches Chaos
101 *stomp sth.* etwas einstampfen / zusammentreten
103–104 *kick the Jesus out of sth.* (infml AE) kick sth. hard
110 *sockdolager* [sɑːk'dɑːlɪdʒər] (AE sl) outstanding, perfect
113 *slimy* (infml) false, imprecise and dishonest
114 *grip sth.* grasp sth., hold sth. tightly
114 *paw sb.* jdn. betatschen / begrapschen
114 *maul sb.* (of a dog) attack and injure sb.
114 *massage sb.* (hier) jdn. duchkneten
114 *pound sb.* hit sb. hard
119 *spoon sth. into sth. else* use a spoon to put sth. into sth. else
119 *transmitter* equipment for sending radio or television signals
124 *figure* think
130 *cackle* make unpleasant noises
135 *bolt* Ballen
135 *feeling of* (here) enjoying
136 *flannel* type of soft light cloth

"Go on."

"Then I got the idea of the portable diathermy machine. I rented one, took it on the bus going home that night. There sat all the tired commuters with their wrist radios, talking to their wives, saying, 'Now I'm at Forty third, now I'm at Forty-fourth, here I am at Forty-ninth, now turning at Sixty-first.' One husband cursing, 'Well, get *out* of that bar, darn it, and get home and get dinner started, I'm at Seventieth!' And the transit-system radio playing 'Tales from the Vienna Woods,' a canary singing words about a first-rate wheat cereal. Then – I switched on my diathermy! Static! Interference! All wives cut off from husbands grousing about a hard day at the office. All husbands cut off from wives who had just seen their children break a window! The 'Vienna Woods' chopped down, the canary mangled! *Silence!* A terrible, unexpected silence. The bus inhabitants faced with having to converse with each other. Panic! Sheer, animal panic!"

"The police seized you?"

"The bus *had* to stop. After all, the music was being scrambled, husbands and wives *were* out of touch with reality. Pandemonium, riot, and chaos. Squirrels chattering in cages! A trouble unit arrived, triangulated on me instantly, had me reprimanded, fined, and home, minus my diathermy machine, in jig time."

"Mr. Brock, may I suggest that so far your whole pattern here is not very – practical? If you didn't like transit radios or office radios or car business radios, why didn't you join a fraternity of radio haters, start petitions, get legal and constitutional rulings? After all, this *is* a democracy."

"And I," said Brock, "am that thing called a minority. I *did* join fraternities, picket, pass petitions, take it to court. Year after year I protested. Everyone laughed. Everyone else *loved* bus radios and commercials. I was out of step."

"Then you should have taken it like a good soldier, don't you think? The majority rules."

"But they went too far. If a little music and 'keeping in touch' was charming, they figured a lot would be ten times as charming. I went *wild*! I got home to find my wife hysterical. *Why*? Because she had been completely out of touch with me for half a day. Remember, I did a dance on my wrist radio? Well, that night I laid plans to murder my house."

"Are you *sure* that's how you want me to write it down?"

"That's semantically accurate. Kill it dead. It's one of those talking, singing, humming, weather-reporting, poetry-reading, novel-reciting, jingle-jangling, rockaby-crooning-when-you-go-to-bed houses. A house that screams opera to you in the shower and teaches you Spanish in your sleep. One of those blathering caves where all kinds of electronic Oracles make you feel a trifle larger than a thimble, with stoves that say, 'I'm apricot pie, and I'm *done*,' or 'I'm prime roast beef, so *baste* me!' and other nursery gibberish like that. With beds that rock you to sleep and *shake* you awake. A house that *barely* tolerates humans, I tell you. A front

139 *diathermy machine* ['daɪə,θɜːmi] machine that generates high-frequency currents
144 *darn it!* (infml AE) damn it!
145 *Tales from the Vienna Woods* a Viennese waltz by Johann Strauss II
147 *static* elements that disturb radio and other signals
147 *interference* interruption, disturbance
147–148 *grouse about sb./sth.* (infml) über jdn./etwas meckern
149–150 *chop sth. down* cut sth. (esp. trees) down
150 *mangle sth.* crush sth. so that it is badly damaged
154 *scramble* vermengen, durcheinander bringen
155 *pandemonium* chaos with a lot of noise and confusion
155 *riot* violent protest
157 *triangulate on sb.* jdn. in die Zange nehmen
157 *reprimand sb.* (fml) give sb. an official warning
157 *fine sb.* make sb. pay money as a punishment
158 *in jig time* in a very short time
161 *fraternity* people sharing the same interests and beliefs
165 *picket* (v) stand somewhere to protest about sth.
165 *pass petitions* Petitionen verabschieden
176 *semantic* related to the meaning of words and sentences
178 *jingle-jangle* produce simple, catchy melodies
178 *rockaby* (hier) schaukeln
178 *croon* sing softly
180 *blather on* (infml) talk continously about trivial things
180 *oracle* (in ancient

door that barks: 'You've mud on your feet, sir!' And an electronic vacuum hound that snuffles around after you from room to room, inhaling every fingernail or ash you drop. Jesus God, *I* say, Jesus God!"

"Quietly," suggested the psychiatrist.

"Remember that Gilbert and Sullivan song – 'I've Got It on My List, It Never Will Be Missed'? All night I listed grievances. Next morning early I bought a pistol. I *purposely* muddied my feet. I stood at our front door. The front door shrilled, 'Dirty feet, muddy feet! Wipe your feet! Please be *neat*!' I shot the damn thing in its keyhole. I ran to the kitchen, where the stove was just whining, 'Turn me *over*!' In the middle of a mechanical omelet I did the stove to death. Oh, how it sizzled and screamed, 'I'm *shorted*!' Then the telephone rang like a spoiled brat. I shoved it down the Insinkerator. I must state here and now I have *nothing* whatever against the Insinkerator; it was an innocent bystander. I feel sorry for it now, a practical device indeed, which never said a word, purred like a sleepy lion most of the time, and digested our leftovers. I'll have it restored. Then I went in and shot the televisor, that insidious beast, that Medusa, which freezes a billion people to stone every night, staring fixedly, that Siren which called and sang and promised so much and gave, after all, so little, but myself always going back, going back, hoping and waiting until – bang! Like a headless turkey, gobbling, my wife whooped out the front door. The Police came. Here I *am*!"

He sat back happily and lit a cigarette.

"And did you realize, in committing these crimes, that the wrist radio, the broadcasting transmitter, the phone, the bus radio, the office intercoms, all were rented or were someone else's property?"

"I would do it all over again, so help me God."

The psychiatrist sat there in the sunshine of that beatific smile.

"You don't want any further help from the Office of Mental Health? You're ready to take the consequences?"

"This is only the beginning," said Mr. Brock. "I'm the vanguard of the small public which is tired of noise and being taken advantage of and pushed around and yelled at, every moment music, every moment in touch with some voice somewhere, do this, do that, quick, quick, now here, now there. You'll see. The revolt begins. My name will go down in history!"

"Mmm." The psychiatrist seemed to be thinking.

"It'll take time, of course. It was all so enchanting at first. The very *idea* of these things, the practical uses, was wonderful. They were almost toys, to be played with, but the people got too involved, went too far, and got wrapped up in a pattern of social behavior and couldn't get out, couldn't admit they were *in*, even. So they rationalized their nerves as something else. 'Our modern age,' they said. 'Conditions,' they said. 'High-strung,' they said. But mark my words, the seed has been sown. I got world-wide coverage on TV, radio, films; *there's* an irony for you. That was five days ago. A billion people know about me. Check your financial

Greece) godly advice and prophecies
181 *a trifle* slightly
181 *thimble* Fingerhut
182 *baste sth.* mit Fett/Bratensaft begießen
183 *gibberish* (infml) nonsense
185 *bark* give orders in an unfriendly way
186 *snuffle* sniff in a noisy way
189 *Gilbert and Sullivan* British composers of popular musical theatre pieces in the 19th century
190 *grievance* reason for complaint or unhappiness
191 *muddy sth.* make sth muddy or dirty
194 *whine* winzeln
195 *sizzle* brutzeln, zischen
196 *spoiled* verwöhnt
196 *brat* (infml) badly behaved child
198 *bystander* onlooker, witness
201 *televisor* (here) television
201 *insidious* heimtückisch
202 *Medusa* (in ancient Greek mythology) a woman with snakes instead of hair who turned people who looked at her into stone
203 *siren* ['saɪrən] woman-like creature whose singing tempted sailors to leave their course and to suffer shipwreck
205 *gobble* kollern
220 *vanguard* first person in or leader of a movement
227 *enchanting* (adj) attractive, delightful
233 *high-strung* nervous, anxious
233 *mark my words* pay attention to what I am saying
233 *sow sth. (sowed – sown)* etwas säen

columns. Any day now. Maybe today. Watch for a sudden spurt, a rise in sales for French chocolate ice cream!"

"I see," said the psychiatrist.

"Can I go back to my nice private cell now, where I can be alone and quiet for six months?"

"Yes," said the psychiatrist quietly.

"Don't worry about me," said Mr. Brock, rising. "I'm just going to sit around for a long time stuffing that nice soft bolt of quiet material in both ears."

"Mmm," said the psychiatrist, going to the door.

"Cheers," said Mr. Brock.

"Yes," said the psychiatrist.

He pressed a code signal on a hidden button, the door opened, he stepped out, the door shut and locked. Alone, he moved in the offices and corridors. The first twenty yards of his walk were accompanied by "Tambourine Chinois." Then it was "Tzigane," Bach's "Passacaglia" and Fugue in something Minor, "Tiger Rag," "Love Is Like a Cigarette." He took his broken wrist radio from his pocket like a dead praying mantis. He turned in at his office. A bell sounded; a voice came out of the ceiling, "Doctor?"

"Just finished with Brock," said the psychiatrist.

"Diagnosis?"

"Seems completely disorientated, but convivial. Refuses to accept the simplest realities of his environment and work *with* them."

"Prognosis?"

"Indefinite. Left him enjoying a piece of invisible material."

Three phones rang. A duplicate wrist radio in his desk drawer buzzed like a wounded grasshopper. The intercom flashed a pink light and click-clicked. Three phones rang. The drawer buzzed. Music blew in through the open door. The psychiatrist, humming quietly, fitted the new wrist radio to his wrist, flipped the intercom, talked a moment, picked up one telephone, talked, picked up another telephone, talked, picked up the third telephone, talked, touched the wrist-radio button, talked calmly and quietly, his face cool and serene, in the middle of the music and the lights flashing, the two phones ringing again, and his hands moving, and his wrist radio buzzing, and the intercoms talking, and voices speaking from the ceiling. And he went on quietly this way through the remainder of a cool, air-conditioned, and long afternoon; telephone, wrist radio, intercom, telephone, wrist radio, intercom, telephone, wrist radio, intercom, telephone, wrist radio, intercom, telephone, wrist radio, intercom, telephone, wrist radio ...

236 *spurt* outbreak of activity, effort, emotion
253 *mantis (= praying mantis)* (Insekt) Gottesanbeterin
258 *convivial* cheerful and friendly

Assignments

1 Outline the various stages of Mr. Brock's case history.

2 List all the gadgets mentioned in the text, describe their functions and their impact on Mr. Brock.

3 Analyze the imagery used in the text.

4 Assess the importance of Mr. Brock's dream of "being a writer" (l. 60) for his behavior.

5 Describe how Brock and the psychologist are characterized and examine the adequacy of their ascribed roles.

6 Imagine you are a lawyer and you have to defend Mr. Brock in court. Find arguments why Mr. Brock should plead "not guilty".

7 Either:

a) Compile information on the music titles mentioned in the short story. Comment on the selection and evaluate the impact of this constant acoustic stream on people's understanding of music.

Or:

b) Produce a musical collage either based on the titles referred to in "The Murderer" or of your own choice, in which you blend in the various styles of music in interesting ways. Present and explain your collage in class.

8 Either:

a) Have you got an mp3 player? If so, assess how and why you use it. Compare the role music plays in the short story to the way it plays a role in your life.

Or:

b) Keep a record of where and when you are exposed to music. Report about the various situations and your feelings.

9 Describe the following painting Max Schlüter's "Young Woman on the Telephone" (1912). Invent a telephone conversation the woman might have.

Then look at the photo of the people with the mobile phones. Write down what they may be talking about.

Post-reading Activities

1 Either:

a) Imagine a day without electricity in your household. Write a diary entry reporting on the greatest difficulties you and your family faced. Include thoughts and emotions

Or:

b) Imagine or experience a weekend without phones, TV, VCR, DVD-player, computer, play station; write a (fictitious) personal report.

2 Look again at your definition of science fiction (cf. p. 4).

a) Describe what elements both stories have in common.

b) Analyze where and when the stories are set.

c) Find a definition of the word "extrapolation" and decide to what extent the author extrapolates developments from his time to create these stories.

3 Read the following information about mobile phone use in Great Britain.

Mobile phones are one of the most widely used of the contemporary ICT. The first digital mobile phone was introduced in the UK in 1991. [...]

The 2006 Media Literacy Audit found a strong link between a mobile phone user's age and the reasons for owning a mobile phone. Adults aged 55 and over were likely to have a mobile phone for use in emergency, while people aged under 35 were likely to acquire a mobile phone for keeping in touch with friends and family and the younger adults, aged under 25, acquired their mobile phone for the purpose of texting. [...]

The range of functions available on mobile phones continues to develop. In January to April 2006, 30 per cent of households in Great Britain possessed a mobile phone that could access the Internet. This was up from 20 per cent in April 2003. In January to April 2006, 11 per cent of adults had used a mobile phone to browse the Internet in the three months before interview.

Another function available on mobile phones is the Short Messaging Service (SMS), also known as texting, which was introduced in 1994. This allows a mobile phone user to send and receive a short written message from other mobile phones. In July 2005, 66 per cent of adults in Great Britain had sent a text, and 68 per cent had received one. Mobile phone users can also receive texts as part of an information service, for example, news headlines, traffic updates, or sports information. In July 2005, 7 per cent of adults subscribed to such services. As well as voice and text, mobile phones that include Multimedia Messaging Service (MMS) can also send pictures. In July 2005, 28 per cent of adults had sent a digital photograph using their mobile phone and 27 per cent had received one. Other functions that are available on some mobile phones, or are being developed, include games, radio, music and television.

The most common reasons why adult mobile phone users in the UK used a mobile phone in 2005, according to the 2006 Media Literacy Audit, were making personal or business calls (85 per cent of mobile phone users) and sending personal or business text messages (70 per cent). However, these uses differed according to age; 94 per cent of young people aged between 16 and 24 sent personal or business text messages compared with 17 per cent of those aged 65 and over.

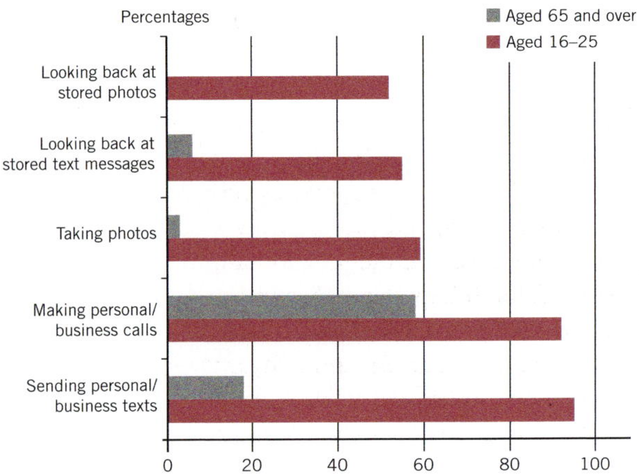

Different uses of mobile phone: by selected age groups, 2005
United Kingdom

Source: 2006 Media Literacy Audit, Ofcom

From: *Vivienne Avery et al.* ***Focus on the Digital Age*** *(2007) at www.statistics.gov.uk/downloads/theme_compendia/foda2007/FocusOnDA.pdf;*

a) Look at the last sentence of the text and compare it to the information in the graph. Then express the rest of the graph in words.

b) Compare the use of mobile phones in Britain with the way you and your fellow students use mobile phones.

c) What else would you like to do with your mobile?

4 Go to the official website of the ARD, find the link "ARD intern" and then "Medien Basisdaten" (*www.ard.de/intern/basisdaten/-/id=8192/18dpbsO/index.html*). Use the charts there to present a short survey of media habits in Germany. Focus especially on young people.

Additional Texts

1 The Need for New Gadgets ADI IGNATIUS

Not long ago I went to see the Celtics play the Jazz at Boston's Fleet Center. I wanted to experience ChoiceSeat, one of the new-generation computers that U.S. sports arenas are installing to give fans an "interactive" experience at the game. It took a while to get comfortable (like about the first quarter), but I finally started making headway with the machine at my seat. You can follow the game (why watch the real thing when you can see it on a tiny screen!), access player stats and pull up background news and video. The coolest application is a function that lets you watch the game from any of 12 angles – you decide which one. Moreover, you can call up instant replays at any time, from any of those 12 vantage points.

This is a case of interactive technology actually filling a need. Sports on TV is all about replays; in fact, viewers get lazy, realizing they don't need to fully concentrate because the key moments will be shown again. When you're at the game, you don't have that luxury, and you can miss a lot. Unless, that is, you're sitting with a ChoiceSeat. In the second half, the Jazz's John Starks suddenly falls to the floor. It happens so fast, most of the 18,000 people in the arena don't notice. With a few clicks I'm able to see, over and over, from 12 different positions, that Boston's Bryant Stith clearly stuck a finger in Starks' eye. "This is starting to make some sense," remarks my initially skeptical companion, Howard Manly, a former sportswriter at the *Boston Globe*.

But we soon encounter the technology's limitation. After a steal, Boston's Paul Pierce viciously slam-dunks over the Jazz defense. Only, I'm busy staring at the box. Suddenly 18,000 fans are on their feet, roaring their approval while I'm trying to find the reset button. I am at the game, with enhanced interactive technology, and I feel like I'm missing the whole thing. ChoiceSeat's motto is: "Get closer." So why do I feel the opposite is happening? When the game ends and the Celtics pull off an upset, a female Jazz fan sitting beside me, wearing a John Stockton T-shirt, unleashes a deafening primal scream. Now that's interactive.

This is how it goes with technology. Every invention is accompanied by passionate claims for its sensational applications. What follows is an inevitable period of adjustment: How do I actually use this thing, anyway? [...]

Still, so many of the technologies that promote interactivity don't fulfill that promise. When I attended the World Economic Forum in Davos, Switzerland, this January, Compaq gave each delegate a free iPaq pocket computer. I sat with a friend and marveled at the gizmo. Then we

1 *Celtics, Jazz* famous Boston and Utah basketball teams
5 *make headway* vorankommen
7 *stats* statistics
11 *vantage point* perspective
23 *steal* (n) taking the ball from the opponent team
24 *slam-dunk* (v) (in basketball) score by jumping in the air and throwing the ball through the basket with your hands over the rim
30 *pull off an upset* eine unerwartetete Niederlage bereiten
31 *John Stockton* famous basketball player
39 *iPaq* type of pocket PC

sent each other e-mails. Hey! Of course, we were sitting side by side (at an indescribably dull panel on Asian economies). Pointless communication, yes, but isn't that what we do nowadays? Think how commonly we send e-mails to colleagues at work who might be as near as the end of our cubicle. Is technology enhancing our ability to interact, or blocking it?

Many of the innovations that get us excited seem to be a drag on the human evolutionary scale. Once upon a time kids just went out and played ball with one another. Eventually computer games allowed us to sit in our rooms and play virtual baseball. Progress! With the Internet, kids can now compete against other players online, in real time! Interactivity! What's next? Some day someone will figure out a way to truly experience the "feel" of throwing and catching a virtual ball remotely, through complicated algorithms developed by Indian software engineers (who, by the way, play cricket) that replicate "force feedback" as encountered in real life. Then we'll almost be back to square one.

It's too easy, of course, to be a skeptic, to regard each new invention with a sense of "wise" detachment and, while praising its state-of-the-art capabilities, wonder aloud if we really need it. But even if we like to wax on about that dusty old Remington typewriter we still love, few among us really want to adopt Luddite lifestyles. And we'd risk missing real progress if we did. The same digital innovations that are incrementally enhancing the realms of sex, sports and entertainment are also changing our world in profound ways. Doctors can conduct surgery remotely, controlling robotic hands from great distances. Quadriplegics can move their paralyzed limbs, implanted with sensors, just by focusing their brain waves. The faithful can find like-minded believers in a persecution – free online environment that can be as anonymous as anyone wishes. These applications are proof of the wonders of our new world, one in which people live longer, healthier, happier lives.

***From:** Adi Ignatius, "We have contact: Is interactive technology uniting the world, or pushing us apart?", in: **Time**, 4 June 2001*

47 *cubicle* abgegrenzter Arbeitsplatz
51 *drag* (n) thing that makes progress difficult
68 *replicate sth.* create a copy of sth. artificially
69 *force feedback* sense of vibration or other motions conveyed to the user of advanced technology
72 *detachment* (inner) distance to sth.
72 *state-of-the-art* (adj) based on the most recent and advanced development
73–74 *wax on about sth.* talk about sth. for a long time in a nostalgic way
75 *Luddite* person who is radically opposed to new technological inventions, named after Ned Lud, who was one of the workers who destroyed machines at the beginning of the Industrial Revolution
76 *incremental* increasing step by step
79 *quadriplegic* (n) [ˌkwɑːdrɪ'pliːdʒɪk] person unable to use their arms and legs

1 Discuss the question – "Is interactive technology uniting the world, or pushing us apart?" – in a written essay. Refer to ideas in the text and to your own ideas.

2 Look at the photos on p. 30 and explain the difference between watching a match live and on TV.

2 Second Life Affair Leads to Couple's Real-Life Divorce

STEVEN MILLER

For its many devotees, the Second Life virtual world is a placc where the everyday constraints of normal life drop away and vivid fantasies can be played out.

But fact and fiction have collided for a British couple who are divorcing after the wife discovered her husband's online alter-ego – a goatee-bearded, medallion wcaring hombrc – called Dave Barmy – with another woman, also virtual.

Amy Taylor, who in Second Life is a club DJ called Laura Skye, said yesterday that as far as she was concerned her husband, David Pollard, was having a real relationship with the human controlling her rival. "It may have started online but it existed entirely in the real world and it hurts just as much," she said. "His was the ultimate betrayal. He had been lying to me."

Second Life is the brainchild of an American company, Linden Lab. Players create a virtual alter ego, or avatar, which can move around the imagined world, meet people, socialise, and buy land and property and set up businesses with the game's virtual currency.

Role-playing games have won plaudits for connecting people, academics and businesses, but the British charity Relate last night said that its counsellors were coming across an increasing number of people whose real-life relationships were falling apart because of what was happening in their parallel, unreal, worlds.

Second Life players have spotted the trend and some have set themselves up as virtual private eyes who check on the fidelity of suspected cyber cheats, or act as virtual relationship counsellors.

Amy Taylor (she has already changed her name by deed poll), 28, and David Pollard, 40, met in an Internet chatroom. She moved from her home in London to be with him in Newquay, Cornwall, and at first they had fun together, in real life and cyberspace.

In Second Life Taylor liked to wear tight-fitting cowboy outfits and she lived by the motto: "Never give your heart easily." Pollard set himself up in a winter chalet with a Cobra helicopter gunship parked next to it. Their avatars became partners in Second Life, until Taylor woke from an afternoon nap and found Pollard at the computer watching his Dave Barmy character having sex with a prostitute.

1 *devotee* fan, follower
5 *alter ego* (n) a person whose personality is different from yours, yet acts as another side of your personality
6 *goatee-bearded* ziegenbärtig
6 *hombre (Spanish)* man (esp. with bad taste)
15 *avatar* (n) (here) the computer representative of sb.
18 *plaudits* (n) praise, approval, applause
24 *private eye* detective
26 *change one's name by deed poll* seinen Namen durch rechtsgültige Erklärung ändern

The real life couple and the Second Life couple

Horrified, Taylor ended the online relationship between Skye and Barmy but stayed with Pollard in real life.

It was then that fact and fiction really began to collide. Taylor decided to test Dave Barmy, and thus Pollard's loyalty, by turning to a virtual female private eye called Markie Macdonald.

A "honeytrap" was set up in which an alluring avatar chatted Barmy up. He passed the test with flying colours, talking about Laura Skye all night.

Barmy and Skye got back together in cyberspace, marrying in a ceremony held in a pretty, tropical grove.

In real life at their flat in Cornwall, Taylor wept as she watched the service and in 2005, in real life again, the couple married in the less glamorous surroundings of St Austell register office.

But Taylor sensed something was wrong and eventually she found Barmy chatting affectionately in Second Life to a woman who was not Skye.

She found it even more disturbing than his earlier tryst as there seemed genuine affection in it. In real life, she filed for divorce.

Taylor said she realised the saga sounded "bizarre" but added: "People find love in lots of different ways."

She said she still played Second Life, and there was a chance her alter ego would bump into her former partner's. It would be awkward, but they would survive.

Pollard admitted he was having an online relationship with an American woman. "We weren't even having cyber sex or anything like that, we were just chatting and hanging out together. It was nothing really major. I don't think I was really doing anything wrong."

From: *Steven Morris,* ***The Guardian****, 14 November 2008*

41 *alluring* (adj) attractive
45 *grove* small group of trees
48 *register office* Standesamt
52 *tryst* secret rendezvous

1 a) Contrast the real life couple and their Second Life counterpartners based on what you read in the text and gather from the photos.
b) Speculate on people's motives for leading "virtual" lives.

2 Write a short story based on the events of the report.

3 Provide a survey of the most popular video and computer games, in which you:
– explain their content and rules;
– point out potential dangers of these virtual worlds, especially for young people.

4 According to the catharsis theory, escaping into virtual worlds might actually be therapeutic, as watching and using violence in virtual worlds may help to channel aggressive feelings in harmless ways and prevent us from using violence in the real world. Do research on this theory and then comment on it.

3 The Amtrak Quiet Car: Where Silence Sells KARL VILACOBA

My Tuesday morning train ride felt like it broke new ground for the rudeness of fellow passengers. At one point, there must have been a half-dozen cell phone conversations going on in my direct comfort zone, a maddening feeling for a guy who depends on that extra hour of pre-work shuteye.

On my train, people who loudly subject the rest of us to the unimportant details of their lives are usually scorned. I've seen out-of-hand cell phone talkers heckled, confronted and, in one case, even given a round of applause by a whole car full of riders once his conversation was done. But on this morning, it seemed the rules of commuter etiquette were collectively thrown out the vestibule. [...]

Out of curiosity, I searched around the Web the other day to see if any companies or transit agencies had come up with any interesting rules regarding cell phone abuse, and I came across a very novel approach being taken by Amtrak. In late 1999, a group of frustrated regular riders of the Philadelphia to Washington, D.C., morning train banded together and requested a car be set aside as a sanctuary from the beeps, blabbing and Beethoven symphonies. The Quiet Car soon became a reality and a patented concept.

The Quiet Car's success shows not only that silence is a virtue, but silence sells.

"It has been popular enough that we've extended the Quiet Car to several Amtrak trains," said Tracy Connell, a spokesperson for Amtrak. "I don't have any stats on it, but I know the response has been very positive and we've had a lot of compliments on it."

• *Amtrak* name of the US national railroad company
8 *heckle* interrupt sb. by shouting out rude remarks
17 *sanctuary* asylum

Quiet Car rules state that riders may not use any noise-making devices such as cell phones, pagers, laptops with audible features enabled, or handheld games and music players without headphones. Conversation must be kept in quiet, subdued tones. Conductors are instructed to ask anyone who disregards these rules to leave the car, Connell said.

The Quiet Car seems like a sensible way for Amtrak to balance the needs of riders seeking peace and quiet with those of business travelers who have work to do that requires their being in touch with the outside world. It also addresses a problem that will only get worse. At the time those passengers first took a stand in 1999, about 86 million people had cell phone subscriptions in the U.S., according to CTIA-The Wireless Association, an organization representing members of the wireless telecommunications industry. That number has since nearly tripled to about 254 million subscribers today.

So what's the lesson here? If you're looking for some peace and quiet on your commute, your best bet may be to gather up some friends and ask for it. Just please don't do it over your cell phone, sitting next to me.

27 *pager* Funkmeldeempfänger, Piepser

From: *Karl Vilacoba,* ***The Intransition Blog****, http://intransitionmag.blogspot.com/2008/02/amtrack-quiet-car-where-silence-sells.html, 4 February 2008*

1 Sum up the main ideas of the blog.

2 Imagine you want to organize a travellers' initiative proposing Deutsche Bahn AG to introduce Quiet Cars. Draft a pamphlet in which you describe the concept of the Quiet Car and justify your demand.

3 Discuss whether the idea behind the Quiet Car might have been used as an alternative solution in Ray Bradbury's short story "The Murderer".

4 Daring to Seek Silence, and Ideas, in the Wired World's Din

CLYDE HABERMAN

You see them by the thousands: New Yorkers walking along the street plugged into everything imaginable. Everything, that is, except themselves.

They are hooked to iPods. They punch away at BlackBerries. They yak on their cellphones.

Whatever pleasure or benefit they derive from this, one thing they are almost certainly not doing is thinking freely, letting their minds wander. You wonder what eureka moment may have been missed in all this busyness. Did the world lose the cure for cancer? Or the plot for a great novel?

5 *yak (infml)* talk continuously about unimportant things
8 *eureka moment* [ju'ri:kə] happy moment when you have a sudden answer to a problem

Her feelings exactly, said Julie Mehretu, a Manhattan artist. "I don't walk around the street with an iPod or cellphone," she said. "Idle time is used by me to think things out."

Teresita Fernandez, a New York sculptor, agrees. "I'm a great believer in daydreaming," she said. "I think it's a very powerful private moment that's loaded with information." Her cellphone stays off when she is out and about.

Last month Ms. Mehretu and Ms. Fernandez were among the men and women named recipients of MacArthur Fellowships, the so-called genius grants, worth $500,000 and awarded each year by the John D. and Catherine T. MacArthur Foundation of Chicago.

MacArthur fellows are nearly unanimous on being unwired for creativity.

"Nonconnectivity becomes a commodity, something to cherish," said Jonathan Lethem, a Brooklyn novelist and a new MacArthur fellow. "You need so much ruminative time to build these elaborate alternate realities. Every novelist is running away from the telephone. Has been for 100 years."

It troubles Majora Carter, a 2005 winner, that many young people are wired all the time. "They don't have the ability anymore to create things in their own head, to create fantasies, to create dreams for themselves," she said.

For that matter, when was the last time that you heard someone whistling sweetly on the street?

New Yorkers are so busy plugging into electronic sources that they have forgotten how to make music for themselves.

From: *Clyde Haberman,* ***The New York Times****, 4 October 2005*

1 Explain what is meant by "nonconnectivity" (l. 31).

2 Compare the individuals mentioned in this text with Mr. Brock in Bradbury's "The Murderer".

3 Most young people do walk around with mp3 players and cellphones. Give reasons why they feel this is preferable to walking around without them.

24 *recipient* receiver
25 *grant* scholarship
31–32 *commodity* sth. that one buys or acquires
32 *cherish sth.* regard as valuable
35 *ruminative* used for thinking

5 The Company that Produces Music DAVID OWEN

The company that became Muzak was founded by George Owen Squier, a career Army officer, who was born in Dryden, Michigan, in 1865. [...] In the early nineteen-hundreds, he invented a system of [...] transmitting multiple radio signals along the outside of electrical, telegraph, and telephone lines. Squier realized that his invention could be used to deliver music, news, and other programming directly to homes and businesses. In 1922 [...] he sold a license to the North American Company, a public-utility conglomerate, which formed a new subsidiary, Wired Radio, to develop the idea. [...] In 1934, Wired Radio – following the example of Eastman's brilliant coinage, Kodak – changed its name to Muzak. Squier died the same year, of pneumonia.

As the quality and quantity of wireless radio broadcasts increased, eliminating the residential market for wired radio, Squier's company concentrated on selling background music to hotels, restaurants, and other businesses, many of them at first in New York City. (Muzak is probably called elevator music because soothing melodies were used in early skyscrapers to make people feel less nervous about stepping into a contrivance that looked like a death trap.) In the forties, Muzak introduced a trademarked concept, called Stimulus Progression, which held that most workers would be more productive if they were exposed to music of gradually increasing intensity, in fifteen-minute cycles. The process was said to be subliminal: Muzak affected you the way hypnosis did, whether you wanted it to or not. [...]

Stimulus Progression acquired a vast supporting apparatus of baffling in-house research studies and impenetrable charts and diagrams. It was pseudoscience, but it remained alive at the company until the late nineties, partly because it was a useful marketing tool and partly because it seemed so plausible: most people really were happier and more productive when there was something humming along in the background. Recorded music was "piped" into insurance offices, ocean liners, hotel lobbies, and department stores, and Muzak built a network of franchisees to spread its business further. Today, the company estimates that its daily audience is roughly a hundred million people, in more than a dozen countries, and that it supplies sixty per cent of the commercial background music in the United States. (Modern Muzak is delivered to customers by satellite, over broadband, and on high-capacity disks.)

Until the late 19th century, people usually had little access to music unless they made the music themselves, and even in the 1920s, when Wired Radio began, most people's lives were still tuneless much of the time. Muzak's early listeners didn't have clock radios, car CD players, MTV, home entertainment centers, in-flight hip-hop programs, satellite radio, or iPods, and when their telephone rang it didn't play the theme to "The Godfather." Muzak, for many people, was the first manifestation of a phenomenon that is now so familiar we scarcely notice it: the shifting, and frequently inescapable, soundtrack of everyday life. [...]

8 *subsidiary* Tochterunternehmen
18 *contrivance* [kən'traɪvəns] complicated device made for a particular purpose
22 *subliminal* that influences you even though you are not aware of it
25 *baffling (adj)* confusing
25 *impenetrable* impossible to understand
31 *franchise* Lizenzunternehmen

During Muzak's early decades, office workers and others sometimes complained that public background music was an invasion of privacy. Some people feel that way today, although the first thing many of us do when we find ourselves alone with our thoughts is to reach for the handiest means of drowning them out – by putting on a pair of headphones, say, or by sliding a disk into the car's CD player. Audio architecture is a compelling concept because the human response to musical accompaniment is powerful and involuntary. "Our biggest competitor," a member of Muzak's marketing department told me, "is silence."

From: *David Owen, "Annals Of Culture – The Soundtrack Of Your Life: Muzak in the realm of retail theatre",* ***The New Yorker****, 10 April 2006*

1 Explain the term "audio architecture".

2 Comment on the Muzak employee's statement: "Our biggest competitor is silence." (ll. 53–54). Refer to "The Murderer" to illustrate your arguments.

3 In group work, file a complaint against Muzak to an International Human Rights Organization on the basis that silence is a human right. Justify your complaint referring to social, personal, cultural and political arguments.

6 Feierabend ADAM SOBOCZYNSKI

This text is taken from a German newspaper. Read the text and understand its contents so that you would be able to explain what it says to a non-German friend.

Jede Nachricht ist potenziell eine schlechte. Für jene, die ohnehin zu kleinen Neurosen neigen, führen Mailboxnachrichten und E-Mails, die Archive unseres Selbst, zu einer beständigen Unruhe. Zur Sucht ohnehin, da jederzeit eine Neuigkeit darauf warten könnte, von uns entdeckt zu werden. Das neue Heroin heißt iPhone, jenes ultimative Handy, über das man auch Mails abrufen kann, ein Arbeitsgerät, das sich als Technikspielzeug tarnt.

Wie kurzmitteilungsfrei einst die Sonntage waren! Der Feierabend erstreckte sich über den ganzen langen Tag. Auch heute schläft man an diesem Tag zwar aus, geht dann mit seiner Freundin irgendwo frühstücken, aber spätestens am Nachmittag verschränkt sich die Faulenzerei bereits mit kleinen dienstlichen Angelegenheiten, eine Mail am Notebook auf dem Balkon, der kurze Anruf eines Kollegen in der Sonne, am Ende des Tages ahnt man gar nicht mehr, dass man eigentlich gearbeitet hat.

Früher indes war man zur rentnerhaften Ruhe sonntags regelrecht gezwungen. Sonntags schaute man nach der Tagesschau den Tatort. War das Bild dunkel, klingelte das Telefon des Kommissars. Der Kommissar knipste die Nachttischlampe an, sagte sehr müde: "Ja?" Und irgendwo war ein Mord passiert, und er musste sich anziehen und den Tatort sichten, mitten in der Nacht, ein Partisan der Arbeit, immer zur Stelle. Unermüdlich im Einsatz waren ansonsten nur Professor Brinkmann aus der Schwarzwaldklinik und seine Artverwandten. Wenn einer abends oder wochenends arbeitete, ging es stets um Leben und Tod.

Heute haben sich die Kommissare und Ärzte, die einst eine Sonderexistenz führten, auf unheimliche Weise vermehrt. Sie sind aus dem Fernseher getreten und sitzen sehr spät noch beim Italiener oder in einem ICE von, sagen wir, Hamburg nach Berlin. Heroische Einzelkämpfer diverser Branchen, sie packen zunächst ihr Notebook aus, dann ihr BlackBerry, das Erkennungszeichen der Wichtigen, mit dem diese telefonieren, mailen und Termine planen können. Das BlackBerry verbinden sie mit dem Notebook, um irgendwelche Daten zu synchronisieren. Dann legen sie das Handy neben den Rechner und machen sich an die Arbeit. Es geht nicht um Leben und Tod, sondern um die nächste Kundenpräsentation. Und es nervt die von allerlei Technik Umstellten nur, dass noch immer nicht alle Funklöcher gestopft sind. Wir sind technisch hochgerüstet, wie es einst nur Filmfiguren waren, James Bond etwa, der allerlei futuristisches Gerät mit sich herumtrug schon in den Sechzigern. Das macht den Glanz aller mobilen Geräte aus: Indem sie uns immerzu erreichbar machen, suggerieren sie, dass wir für andere unersetzlich sind. Kaum etwas bekämpft unsere Angst vor der Vergänglichkeit wirkungsvoller.

Ich recherchierte über den Verlust des Feierabends noch spätabends. Kolumnist H. sagte mir beim Weißwein, er glaube schon, dass es den Feierabend noch gebe. Aber nur noch bei den einfachen Leuten. Die Bäckereifachangestellte werde gewiss nicht abends noch vom Bäcker angerufen wegen diesem oder jenem. Es sei denn, sie habe ein Verhältnis mit dem Bäcker. Die Putzfrau werde auch nicht vom Putzkolonnenchef angerufen. Der Feierabend sei heute – wie Übergewicht, Rauchen und schlechte Haut – ein Unterschichtenphänomen.

Das ist nur ein klein wenig zugespitzt. Wer früher Zeit hatte, galt als freier Mensch. Er konnte über seine Zeit verfügen – anders als das niedere Bürgertum, die Arbeiter oder die Sklaven, die Pyramiden bauten oder den Kölner Dom. Das war eine antike Überzeugung, über Jahrhunderte auch eine christliche: Arbeit war ein Fluch, den hatte Adam mit seiner Ursünde auf sich gezogen und auf alle seine Nachkommen, wie Eberhard Straub in seiner Abhandlung Vom Nichtstun schreibt. Ja noch die sozialdemokratisierte Industriegesellschaft hatte die von der Arbeitszeit strikt abgegrenzte "Freizeit" geschaffen; ein Begriff, der heute ähnlich antiquiert klingt wie der "Feierabend" – einst aber war er Inbegriff sozialen Fortschritts.

Heute sind wir selbstverständlich jederzeit für unseren Arbeitgeber verfügbar, vor allem in Berufen, die sich als kreativ (Werbung, Journalismus) oder besonders fortschrittlich begreifen (IT-Branche, Unternehmensberatung). Während der Arbeit wiederum sind wir jederzeit verfügbar für unsere Freunde, Ehepartner oder Eltern, die längst an die Entgrenzung von Freizeit und Arbeit gewöhnt sind: "Ich weiß, du hast zu tun, aber sag mal, kommst du am Wochenende zum Essen?"

[...] Die Geschichte der Moderne ist eine Geschichte der Beschleunigung. Wir erfanden, so der Jenaer Soziologe Hartmut Rosa in seinem Buch Beschleunigung, ja allerhand Apparate, die uns Zeitersparnisse bringen sollten: Den Urlaubsflug buchen wir zu Hause am Computer, und statt umständlich die Post aufzusuchen, schreiben wir eine E-Mail. Und doch haben wir keine Zeit. Weil sich unsere Handlungsmöglichkeiten ständig erweitern. Statt vier Briefe am Tag erhalten wir 50 E-Mails. Die Beschleunigung, sagt Rosa, hat sich verselbstständigt; wir leben in dem Bewusstsein, dass jeder Handyrückruf eigentlich schon immer verspätet ist. Dass andere noch etwas schneller sein könnten als wir selbst.

Wir sind nicht Herr unserer Zeit. Auch wenn uns die Werbung Gegenteiliges verheißt: Vodafone sendet derzeit einen Spot, der einen jungen Mann pendelnd zwischen E-Mail-Schreiben im Büro und einer erotischen Cafébegegnung zeigt. Er sieht nicht gut aus, ziemlich blass. Die Lösung, sagt die Stimme aus dem Off, sei ein Handy mit integriertem E-Mail-Empfang. So ließen sich die Pausen zwischen innigen Küssen sinnvoll mit Beruflichem füllen.

Dass eine konfliktfreie Verschmelzung von Beruf und Liebe utopisch ist, wissen wir. Und manchmal beklagen wir auch wortreich den Stress. Insgeheim aber sind wir ziemlich zufrieden. Schließlich ist kaum etwas schöner, als leicht genervt den Wohnzimmertisch oder die Kneipenrunde zu verlassen, um einen dringenden Anruf entgegenzunehmen. Der Prestigegewinn ist beträchtlich. Wir demonstrieren unsere Arbeit öffentlich, statt im dunklen Arbeitszimmer zu verschwinden. Und nirgendwo wird der Stolz der Arbeit derart gekonnt sichtbar gemacht wie hinter den Schaufenstern von Ladenlokalen, die Freiberufler gemietet haben. Es ist lässig, noch nachts darin herumzulaborieren. An einem Text, einer Werbebroschüre, einem Entwurf für eine Häuserzeile. Die Arbeit ist der sogenannten kreativen Klasse ohnehin nicht lästig, sondern sie wird in einen diffusen Alltag integriert, in dem die klassischen Rollenmuster radikal aufgelöst sind: Es lässt sich oft kaum sagen, ob man im Café einen freundschaftlich oder einen beruflich motivierten Kaffee miteinander trinkt. [...]

Wir können nicht mehr verschwinden, nicht mehr unerreichbar durch eine fremde Stadt flanieren, Hügel hinabschreiten, vier Stunden über einem gottverdammten Buch sitzen, ohne zwischendurch ins Internetcafé zu gehen, wenn wir uns schon dazu durchgerungen haben, das Notebook zu Hause zu lassen oder gar das Handy. Vater würde sich Sorgen machen. Die Partnerin oder der Partner. Und zu irgendeinem Projekt, eigentlich abgeschlossen, gäbe es gewiss noch eine Rückfrage. Warum auch nicht. Wir wissen doch, dass Arbeit uns erfüllt, so sehr, wie es kein Partner vermag. Und kein Kind – ansonsten würden wir mehr Kinder zeugen, mehr Spaziergänge machen, "Muße" hätten wir, auch so ein Wort, das verschwindet. Hätte heute jemand Muße, er wäre nicht stolz darauf, sondern arbeitslos.

Und ist man einmal überrascht von der Leere, die einen überkommt, wenn nichts Dringliches ansteht, dann schreibt man, obgleich es nicht wirklich drängt, abends einem Kollegen, wegen einer Konferenz drei Tage später, die womöglich um einen Tagungsordnungspunkt ergänzt werden könnte. Was er denn davon halte? Wir wissen, dass wir nerven. Nicht nur den Kollegen. Sondern den Freund oder die Freundin, unsere Frau oder unseren Mann, wenn wir nachts noch an den Computer schleichen, obgleich es an der Zeit wäre, dass die Körper zueinanderfinden. [...]

Man sagt uns, wir sollen endlich entspannen. Mit Yoga. Machen wir, um den Preis, dass wir noch weniger Zeit haben. Wir gehören einer neuen Schicht an. Wir sind die jederzeit Belangbaren. Wir sind nie schnell genug, aber wir sind schneller als alle andern. Und darauf sind wir stolz.

***From:** Adam Soboczynski, "Der Feierabend hat Feierabend", **Die Zeit**, 28 August 2008*

1 Explain the meaning of the word "Feierabend" to an English friend.

2 Imagine your friend wants to know what the article is about. Outline the writers' main ideas on the changing value attached to work and leisure and the role of the modern communication gadgets in this process.